GREAT SPORTS MINDS
ATHLETE JOURNAL

THINK. BELIEVE. ACHIEVE.

Ann Zaprazny

Copyright © 2020 Great Sports Minds LLC All Rights Reserved.

Unless otherwise indicated, the information and materials available in this book are the property of the author and are protected under U.S. and foreign copyright, trademark, and other intellectual property laws. You may not reproduce or distribute copies of materials found in this book in any form (including by e-mail or other electronic means) without prior written permission from the author. Requests for permission to reproduce or distribute materials found in the book should be sent to AnnZ@Athletementaltraining.com.

Limit of Liability/Disclaimer of Warranties

The information provided and commented upon in these materials is designed to provide guidance only. Such information, comments, and materials are not to be used as a substitute for professional judgment. The information, comments, and materials are to be used for informational purposes only. Any person consulting these materials is solely responsible for implementation of this guidance as it relates to the particular matter for which the end user refers to these materials. Implied warranties of merchantability and fitness of purpose, if any exist, and all other warranties, expressed or implied, are expressly waived by any user of these materials. The author shall not be liable for any direct, indirect, special, or consequential damages, including, without limitation, attorneys' fees or costs arising from any use of these guides or the information or material contained herein.

ISBN: 978-1-7363372-0-2

This journal belongs to:

_____

Date started: _____

A word that inspires me:

_____

My word is *Champion*.

Champion reflects my commitment to provide champion-level service to my clients so that they can be their best and achieve their dreams.

Acknowledgments

The **Great Sports Minds Athlete Journal** could not have happened without the support of so many people.

To my family: Don, Dana, Jason, and Julia, who provided unwavering support as I worked in my office and held late-night Zoom calls with my niece Kate Guinn. Thank you for your patience and love.

To my niece, Kate Guinn, who was in the trenches, and who took the journal from concept to reality. Your encouragement, research, and support were invaluable.

To every athlete, parent, team, coach, and administrator that I have had the honor to work with since 2016. Your passion for your sport, resilience, and dedication inspire me every day to want to serve at a higher level. Your success and well-being are important to me.

To my professional mentors, Dr. Rob Gilbert, Dr. Tricia Lally, and Dr. Patrick Cohn, you inspired me. Dr. Rob Gilbert changed my life by introducing me to the power of positive psychology when I was a young high school basketball coach. Dr. Tricia Lally for flexibility and support of me as a non-traditional student at Lock Haven University. Dr. Patrick Cohn for training many professionals to work with athletes.

To Ginger Johnson, the master connector. Thank you for sharing your wisdom, enthusiasm, and network to help me advance my goal of creating a generation of confident individuals.

To Linda Rey and my fellow entrepreneurs who encouraged me, mentored me, and helped make this happen, I am forever grateful.

Contents

Welcome — 1

The Winning Formula: 8 Fundamental Questions — 7
- How will you be remembered? 8
- What values drive your actions? 9
- What are your big-dream goals? 11
- What will you NOT do in pursuit of your goals? 12
- Is your self-care adequate? 14
- How will you plan and use your time wisely? 16
- What can you control? 18
- What mental performance skills do you need to improve? 20

Daily Reflection — 21

Online Resources — 149

Quote Acknowledgments — 151

References — 153

About the Author — 155

Welcome

Thank you for purchasing the **Great Sports Minds Athlete Journal**.

Congratulations! You have taken a step to level up your mental performance training.

This journal is for every athlete who has a dream, and for everyone who is training to be the very best they can be.

My name is Ann Zaprazny, the CEO and founder of Great Sports Minds LLC and the **Great Sports Minds Athlete Journal** author. I am a certified Mental Game Coach and Positive Coaching Alliance Trainer. I work with athletes to help transform their confidence so they can achieve their goals.

As a three-sport athlete in high school and a Division I basketball player in college, journaling helped me relieve stress, reflect on past performances, and, most importantly, learn and grow personally and athletically. As a professional, I still journal today!

I know what it's like to achieve success, win a championship, be disappointed, lose a sport to an injury, and more.

The **Great Sports Minds Athlete Journal** can help you be your best as you navigate the challenges of your sport.

The **Great Sports Minds Athlete Journal** consists of three sections:

1. The Winning Formula
2. 90 Daily Reflections
3. 12 Weekly Challenges

The Winning Formula includes eight fundamental questions to challenge you to think about the basics. When you first started your sport, you worked on your fundamental skills. Once you had the fundamentals, you advanced to more challenging skills.

The eight fundamental questions will take you about 45 minutes to complete. You will reflect on your:

1. Legacy
2. Values
3. Goals
4. Discipline
5. Self-Care
6. Time Management
7. Controllables
8. Mental Performance Skills

With the fundamental questions completed, you will advance to the second and third sections: the Daily Reflections and the Weekly Challenges.

Welcome

The Daily Reflection pages consist of seven questions to answer every day. A weekly challenge follows every seventh day.

Daily Reflection and Weekly Challenges

Use the Weekly Reflection page to write about your week: how you are performing, what's going well, and what's getting in your way.

The Weekly Challenges introduce essential mental performance skills, including:

- Finding Your Joy and Passion in Sport
- Using Your Breath to Center and Calm
- Releasing a Poor Performance
- Rewriting Limiting Beliefs
- Letting Go of Unrealistic Expectations
- Commiting to Improvement
- Moving Through Mistakes
- Strategies to Strengthen Your Confidence
- Visualizing Your Success
- Emotional Control in Sport
- How to Mentally Prepare for Sport
- Your Sport and Your Identity

The **Great Sports Minds Athlete Journal** can help you focus, grow, and achieve your goals.

> *The best competition I have is against myself to become better.*
> **— John Wooden**

Why Journal?

I have been studying high performance for many years. I wish I knew what I now know when I was a high school and college athlete: that high performance takes just as much work off the court as it does on it.

Journaling is one step to help you express gratitude, focus on goals, release stress, and establish a plan for your sport.

My Approach

Since 2016, I have worked with athletes to transform their confidence and achieve their goals. It's been rewarding to watch their transformations.

It's imperative to train our minds just like we train our bodies. I have watched athletes make beneficial shifts because they did both the physical and mental work to set goals, reflect, and commit to improving. This journal will help you solidify that process.

My niece, Kate Guinn, a former college athlete, collaborated with me. We incorporated the feedback we received from middle school, high school, college and adult athletes, as well as from parents and coaching staff.

Welcome

I am excited to offer this journal to you. My goal is to provide you with the tools you need to reflect and grow as a person and athlete.

> *Enjoy the little things, for one day you may look back and realize they were the big things.*
> **– Robert Brault**

The time in your life as an athlete is special.

Remember how happy you were when you:

- Made the team?
- Had your first success?
- Had a great training session?
- Celebrated a win with your team?

Embrace those moments. Embrace the small things.

Consistently doing the small things well builds habits that will transform into big things. The practice of daily reflection through journaling is a small step that can lead to your next big step.

Your Commitment

> *We are what we repeatedly do. Excellence, then, is not an act, but a habit.*
> **– Will Durant**

Commit to using the journal every day, even if only for 5 minutes. Transformation can only work if you do the work. Make journaling part of your training regimen.

I, _____ commit to using this journal for the next 90 days to grow as an individual and as an athlete.

Stay well! Compete well!

Ann Zaprazny

P.S. Use #trainthementalgame on social media and let us know how your sport and or your season is going.

The Winning Formula:
8 Fundamental Questions

- Legacy
- Values
- Goals
- Discipline
- Self-Care
- Time Management
- Controllables
- Mental Performance Skills

These eight questions will provide clarity on what is important to you and a foundation for success. The Daily Reflection pages begin after the eight questions.

> *There may be people who have more talent than you do, but there's no excuse for anyone to work harder than you do.*
> **– Derek Jeter**

Question 1
How will you be remembered?

Imagine life years from now when you are ready to transition away from the sport that you have so passionately pursued. What will you be remembered for? What will your legacy be?

_____

_____

_____

_____

_____

_____

_____

_____

_____

The Winning Formula: 8 Fundamental Questions

> *Decisions are easy when your values are clear.*
> **– Unknown**

QUESTION 2
What values drive your actions?

Determine your core values. From the list below, select the values or the words that most resonate with you. Do not overthink your selections.

Select the values that are most true for you:

- ☐ Accountable
- ☐ Calm
- ☐ Cheerful
- ☐ Compassionate
- ☐ Consistent
- ☐ Dedicated
- ☐ Dependable
- ☐ Encouraging
- ☐ Enthusiastic
- ☐ Fun
- ☐ Generous
- ☐ Honest
- ☐ Humble
- ☐ Humorous
- ☐ Intelligent
- ☐ Joyful
- ☐ Kind
- ☐ Knowledgeable
- ☐ Loyal
- ☐ Difference-maker
- ☐ Motivated
- ☐ Optimistic
- ☐ Passionate
- ☐ Proactive
- ☐ Punctual
- ☐ Reliable
- ☐ Resilient
- ☐ Responsible
- ☐ Selfless
- ☐ Thankful
- ☐ Unique

Select what is most important to you:

- ☐ Achievement
- ☐ Balance
- ☐ Being the Best
- ☐ Faith
- ☐ Family
- ☐ Friendships
- ☐ Growth
- ☐ Integrity
- ☐ Leadership
- ☐ Performance
- ☐ Preparation
- ☐ Relationships
- ☐ Self-Control
- ☐ Strategy
- ☐ Teamwork
- ☐ Vision

Of these values or words, the three most important to me are:

1. _____

2. _____

3. _____

My values are important to me as an athlete and a person because:

_____
_____
_____
_____
_____
_____
_____
_____
_____

> *A dream doesn't become a reality through magic; it takes sweat, determination, and hard work.*
> **– Colin Powell**

QUESTION 3
What are your big-dream goals?

Goals are aspirations. They often give us a beacon of light when we need it most. For this exercise, write your goals as if you have already accomplished them and they are true today. Instead of writing, "My goal is to earn a scholarship," write "I am playing on scholarship at the college of my dreams" or "I am enjoying my season to the fullest and contributing at my highest level."

What are your dream goals? (big-picture)

_____

_____

What are your short-term goals? (0-3 months?)

_____

_____

What are your mid-term goals? (3-6months?)

_____

_____

What are your long-term goals? (6-12 months?)

_____

_____

> *Your decisions reveal your priorities.*
> — **Jeff Van Gundy**

Question 4
What will you NOT do in pursuit of your goals?

Having clarity around what behaviors you will NOT be a part of is just as important as goal setting. You choose how you spend your time: what you decide to do, and not to do.

Below is a list of behaviors that can distract or derail you from pursuing your goals.

To achieve your goals and not participate in certain activities requires discipline and self-control. Select the behaviors you will not participate in because your passion and desire to achieve your goals is more significant than any distraction.

- ☐ Arguing with officials/referees
- ☐ Cheating
- ☐ Disrespecting a teammate, coach, opponent, parent
- ☐ Gossiping
- ☐ Posting inappropriate content on social media
- ☐ Stealing
- ☐ Binging TV and social media
- ☐ Drinking
- ☐ Fighting/Losing your Temper
- ☐ Hazing/Bullying
- ☐ Smoking/Vaping
- ☐ Using drugs

Which one of these distractions is the most challenging for you and why?

_____

_____

_____

_____

_____

What will you gain by eliminating or reducing this distraction from your life?

_____

_____

_____

_____

_____

> *To fall in love with yourself is the first secret of happiness.*
> **– Unknown**

QUESTION 5
Is your self-care adequate?

Athletes need self-care to be their best. Athletes can:
- Over train and fail to invest in rest and recovery.
- Ignore the pain of injuries.
- Ignore the impact of illness on their well-being.
- Operate with a constant sleep deficit.
- Fail to fuel and hydrate their body adequately.
- Let a poor performance erase years of training and confidence.
- Let their sport define who they are as a person.
- Overthink their coach's decisions.
- Have false beliefs about their coach or teammate that erodes their confidence.
- Forget to acknowledge that they are still learning and growing in their sport.

I want you to enjoy your sport and commit to optimum mental and physical self-care. Identify the self-care habits you will adopt.

- ☐ Give yourself the grace to fail and learn.
- ☐ Acknowledge that your sport is what you do, not who you are.
- ☐ Acknowledge your pain and injuries and seek treatment when needed.
- ☐ Support your teammates. Together we make the TEAM better.
- ☐ Seek to find enjoyment in each practice.
- ☐ Acknowledge your improvement.
- ☐ Commit to adequate rest and recovery.
- ☐ Talk to your coach to seek clarity.
- ☐ Acknowledge illness and its impact on your body.
- ☐ Commit to 8-10 hours of sleep as much as possible.
- ☐ Commit to fueling and hydrating your body appropriately.

Which self-care habit do you need to spend the most time practicing?

_____

_____

_____

Why is this hard for you?

_____

_____

_____

What will you gain if you improve this self-care habit?

_____

_____

_____

> *There are 86,400 seconds in a day. It's up to you to decide what to do with them.*
> — **Jim Valvano**

QUESTION 6
How will you plan and use your time wisely?

We all have the same amount of time in a day. How we use our time is what separates high achievers from the pack.

According to an ABC News report, American teens spend over 7 hours a day on devices for entertainment. Adults spend nearly an equivalent amount of time in front of screens for work and entertainment. Let that sink in—7 hours per day. That equates to 49 hours per week and 2,548 hours per year. Americans are spending a lot of time on screens.

To be successful, you have to be intentional about how you will use your time.

How will you use your 24 hours? The Centers for Disease Control and Prevention (CDC) recommends 8-10 hours of sleep for youth ages 13-18 and at least 7 hours of sleep for 18- to 60-year-olds. How will you allocate your time to optimize your health and your performance athletically, academically, and personally?

Use the next page to plan a great day. Have fun planning your day!

Plan a Great Day

5 a.m. _____

6 a.m. _____

7 a.m. _____

8 a.m. _____

9 a.m. _____

10 a.m. _____

11 a.m. _____

12 p.m. _____

1 p.m. _____

2 p.m. _____

3 p.m. _____

4 p.m. _____

5 p.m. _____

6 p.m. _____

7 p.m. _____

8 p.m. _____

9 p.m. _____

10 p.m. _____

11 p.m. _____

12 a.m. _____

1 a.m. _____

2 a.m. _____

3 a.m. _____

4 a.m. _____

> *There are many things beyond our control. When you can't control what is happening, control the way you respond to what's happening. That's where your power is.*
> **– Unknown**

QUESTION 7
What can you control?

We all want control. We want control over our performance, control over our scores, control over our amount of playing time, etc.

There are many things that athletes focus on that are beyond their control. Athletes have shared with me they hate competing in cold weather; they hate a specific venue; they hate competing against a particular opponent.

When we focus on what we can't control, we waste energy and stress about things we cannot change. Make a list of the things you CAN NOT CONTROL.

_____

_____

_____

_____

Look at each item on your list. Acknowledge that it is out of your control. Let it go.

The Winning Formula: 8 Fundamental Questions

When we focus on what we can control, our confidence goes up. Examples of things we can control: our preparation and self-care, how we fuel and hydrate our body, our effort at practice, our attitude. Make a list of the things you CAN CONTROL.

_____

_____

_____

_____

LEAD is an acronym that we can use to identify what we can control.

L = Leadership: Lead every day. You do not need a title to be a leader. Lead by being a good teammate, working hard at practice, and respecting your coach, the officials, and opponents.

E = Effort: Bring your best effort and energy to everything you do, even when you don't want to do it.

A= Attitude: Display your best attitude during good times and bad. A positive attitude can have a significant impact on everything you do and achieve.

D= Discipline: Practice discipline by showing up, doing your best, and consistently making the right choices even when you don't want to.

What does it look like when you LEAD effectively?

_____

_____

_____

_____

> *The body is ready. We just need to convince our mind.*
> **– Unknown**

Question 8
What mental performance skills do you need to improve?

If you want to compete at your highest level, you need to learn to master essential mental performance skills. Mindset matters. Your mental performance during competition matters.

You physically train hard, and yet you may struggle with self-doubt, confidence, or emotional control. Sport is both a mental and physical challenge. Most athletes physically train. Few invest and develop their mental performance skills.

Identify the essential mental performance skills you would like to improve:

- ☐ Increase confidence
- ☐ Let go of the fear of failure
- ☐ Improve ability to visualize success
- ☐ Eliminate social comparison
- ☐ Reduce my pre-competition stress/anxiety
- ☐ Improve emotional control
- ☐ Trust in my skills
- ☐ Minimize the need for social approval
- ☐ Stop negative self-talk
- ☐ Let go of and move through mistakes effectively

What is the **ONE** mental Performance skill you want to focus on now? _____

Why is strengthening this skill important?

_____

_____

Daily Reflection

Life is only a reflection of what we allow ourselves to see.
— **Unknown**

Daily Reflection Pages

The journal consists of 90 Daily Reflection pages and 12 Weekly Challenges. The Daily Reflection pages have the following prompts:

What's happening in my life right now? Capture what's going on in your life and/or sport.

What's my dream goal? Write down your goals every day as if you have already achieved them.

What am I grateful for today? Gratitude is important. According to the Greater Good Science Center, increased happiness, positive mood, and greater resilience are among the many benefits of consistently expressing gratitude.

What did I do today that I am proud of? Often, athletes are very tough on themselves. I want you to see the good in your day. Share something positive about your efforts today.

What is one thing I can learn or improve? The best athletes in the world are committed to learning and improving. Make that commitment.

How did I L.E.A.D. today? Share a positive example of your Leadership, Effort, Attitude, or Discipline.

WIN: What's important now? What matters to me today?

After you complete a week of Daily Reflections, you'll complete a Weekly Challenge that introduces essential mental performance skills and provides additional opportunities for refection and growth.

Daily Reflection

Entry: 1
Date: ___/___/___

> *Practice like you've never won. Compete like you've never lost.*
> **– Alex Morgan**

What's happening in my life right now?
_____
_____

What's my dream goal?
_____
_____

What am I grateful for today?
_____
_____

What did I do today that I am proud of?
_____
_____

What is one thing I can learn or improve?
_____
_____

How did I L.E.A.D. today?
_____
_____

WIN: What's important now?
_____
_____

Entry: 2
Date: ___/___/___

> *The more you express gratitude for what you have, the more likely you will have even more to express gratitude for.*
> **– Zig Ziglar**

What's happening in my life right now?
_____
_____

What's my dream goal?
_____
_____

What am I grateful for today?
_____
_____

What did I do today that I am proud of?
_____
_____

What is one thing I can learn or improve?
_____
_____

How did I L.E.A.D. today?
_____
_____

WIN: What's important now?
_____
_____

Daily Reflection

Entry: 3
Date: ___/___/___

> *I think I run my strongest when I run with joy, with gratitude, with focus, with grace.*
> **– Kristin Armstrong**

What's happening in my life right now?
_____
_____

What's my dream goal?
_____
_____

What am I grateful for today?
_____
_____

What did I do today that I am proud of?
_____
_____

What is one thing I can learn or improve?
_____
_____

How did I L.E.A.D. today?
_____
_____

WIN: What's important now?
_____
_____

#TRAINTHEMENTALGAME

Entry: 4
Date: ___/___/___

> *There is always going to be a reason why you can't do something; your job is to constantly look for reasons why you can achieve your dreams.*
> **– Shannon Miller**

What's happening in my life right now?
_____
_____

What's my dream goal?
_____
_____

What am I grateful for today?
_____
_____

What did I do today that I am proud of?
_____
_____

What is one thing I can learn or improve?
_____
_____

How did I L.E.A.D. today?
_____
_____

WIN: What's important now?
_____
_____

Daily Reflection

Entry: 5
Date: ___/___/___

> *Be somebody who makes everyone feel like somebody.*
> **– Unknown**

What's happening in my life right now?
_____
_____

What's my dream goal?
_____
_____

What am I grateful for today?
_____
_____

What did I do today that I am proud of?
_____
_____

What is one thing I can learn or improve?
_____
_____

How did I L.E.A.D. today?
_____
_____

WIN: What's important now?
_____
_____

Entry: 6
Date: ___/___/___

> *You are never really playing an opponent. You are playing yourself, your own highest standards, and when you reach your limits, that is real joy.*
> **– Arthur Ashe**

What's happening in my life right now?
_____
_____

What's my dream goal?
_____
_____

What am I grateful for today?
_____
_____

What did I do today that I am proud of?
_____
_____

What is one thing I can learn or improve?
_____
_____

How did I L.E.A.D. today?
_____
_____

WIN: What's important now?
_____
_____

Daily Reflection

Entry: 7
Date: ___/___/___

> *The player you are today should be able to outplay the player from yesterday.*
> **– Unknown**

What's happening in my life right now?
_____
_____

What's my dream goal?
_____
_____

What am I grateful for today?
_____
_____

What did I do today that I am proud of?
_____
_____

What is one thing I can learn or improve?
_____
_____

How did I L.E.A.D. today?
_____
_____

WIN: What's important now?
_____
_____

WEEKLY REFLECTION

Daily Reflection

> *Find your why and you will find your way.*
> **– John Maxwell**

Challenge 1: Find Your Joy and Passion

Congratulations! You have seven entries and are forming a new habit. Keep up the excellent work.

Why did you choose your sport?

_____

_____

_____

Recall when you first started your sport. Remember when you decided that this was "it" for you. Describe that moment. What emotions do you recall?

_____

_____

_____

When you practice and compete today, do your emotions align with your original experiences?

▫YES   ▫NO

If they do, what do you need to do to maintain the joy and happiness in your sport? If they don't, what's getting in your way?

_____

_____

_____

_____

_____

What must you do differently to have greater joy and happiness in your sport?

_____

_____

_____

_____

_____

Commit to playing for the joy and love of your sport again.

Daily Reflection

Entry: 8
Date: ___/___/___

> *The principle is competing against yourself. It's about self-improvement, about being better than you were the day before.*
> **– Steve Young**

What's happening in my life right now?
_____
_____

What's my dream goal?
_____
_____

What am I grateful for today?
_____
_____

What did I do today that I am proud of?
_____
_____

What is one thing I can learn or improve?
_____
_____

How did I L.E.A.D. today?
_____
_____

WIN: What's important now?
_____
_____

Entry: 9

Date: ___/___/___

> *Do your best. And the most important thing is to have fun.*
> **– Unknown**

What's happening in my life right now?
_____
_____

What's my dream goal?
_____
_____

What am I grateful for today?
_____
_____

What did I do today that I am proud of?
_____
_____

What is one thing I can learn or improve?
_____
_____

How did I L.E.A.D. today?
_____
_____

WIN: What's important now?
_____
_____

Daily Reflection

Entry: 10
Date: ___/___/___

How hard would you play if you knew you couldn't play tomorrow?
— **Michele Keiff**

What's happening in my life right now?
_____
_____

What's my dream goal?
_____
_____

What am I grateful for today?
_____
_____

What did I do today that I am proud of?
_____
_____

What is one thing I can learn or improve?
_____
_____

How did I L.E.A.D. today?
_____
_____

WIN: What's important now?
_____
_____

Entry: 11
Date: ___/___/___

> *The five S's of sports training are stamina, speed, strength, skill, and spirit; but the greatest of these is spirit.*
> **– Ken Doherty**

What's happening in my life right now?
_____
_____

What's my dream goal?
_____
_____

What am I grateful for today?
_____
_____

What did I do today that I am proud of?
_____
_____

What is one thing I can learn or improve?
_____
_____

How did I L.E.A.D. today?
_____
_____

WIN: What's important now?
_____
_____

Daily Reflection

Entry: 12
Date: ___/___/___

> *Passion first, and everything will fall into place.*
> — **Holly Holm**

What's happening in my life right now?
_____
_____

What's my dream goal?
_____
_____

What am I grateful for today?
_____
_____

What did I do today that I am proud of?
_____
_____

What is one thing I can learn or improve?
_____
_____

How did I L.E.A.D. today?
_____
_____

WIN: What's important now?
_____
_____

Entry: 13
Date: ___/___/___

> *Do you know what my favorite part of the game is? The opportunity to play.*
> **- Mike Singletary**

What's happening in my life right now?
_____
_____

What's my dream goal?
_____
_____

What am I grateful for today?
_____
_____

What did I do today that I am proud of?
_____
_____

What is one thing I can learn or improve?
_____
_____

How did I L.E.A.D. today?
_____
_____

WIN: What's important now?
_____
_____

Daily Reflection

Entry: 14
Date: ___/___/___

I believe in the impossible because no one else does.
– Florence Griffith Joyner

What's happening in my life right now?
_____
_____

What's my dream goal?
_____
_____

What am I grateful for today?
_____
_____

What did I do today that I am proud of?
_____
_____

What is one thing I can learn or improve?
_____
_____

How did I L.E.A.D. today?
_____
_____

WIN: What's important now?
_____
_____

WEEKLY REFLECTION

Daily Reflection

> *That breath you just took is a gift.*
> **– Robert Bell**

Challenge 2: Using Your Breath to Center and Calm

You are two weeks into using your journal. Nice job! Keep up the great work!

This week's challenge is about using your breath to center and calm. Sometimes we get very nervous about a big game or competition — so nervous that it impacts our performance. Our hearts can race, and our thoughts can erode our confidence. When this happens, you can use your breath and keyword(s) to help you settle and calm.

How to slow your breath:

- Inhale slowly through your nose to a count of four.
- Feel your breath rise through your belly, your lungs, and your collarbone. Hold your breath for a count of four.
- Exhale through pursed lips to a count of four.

Now, take control of your thoughts by focusing on one word as you inhale and one word as you exhale.

- Example 1: Calm and Confidence
- Example 2: Calm and Trust

How can you use your breath in sport?

_____

_____

_____

_____

How can you use your breath in school or work? Throughout the day?

_____

_____

_____

_____

How can using your breath help you?

_____

_____

_____

_____

Commit to using your breath to center and calm.

Daily Reflection

Entry: 15
Date: ___/___/___

> *Sometimes the most important thing in a whole day is the rest we take between two deep breaths.*
> **– Etty Hillesum**

What's happening in my life right now?
_____
_____

What's my dream goal?
_____
_____

What am I grateful for today?
_____
_____

What did I do today that I am proud of?
_____
_____

What is one thing I can learn or improve?
_____
_____

How did I L.E.A.D. today?
_____
_____

WIN: What's important now?
_____
_____

Entry: 16
Date: ___/___/___

> *Breathe, it's just a bad day, not a bad life.*
> **— Unknown**

What's happening in my life right now?
_____
_____

What's my dream goal?
_____
_____

What am I grateful for today?
_____
_____

What did I do today that I am proud of?
_____
_____

What is one thing I can learn or improve?
_____
_____

How did I L.E.A.D. today?
_____
_____

WIN: What's important now?
_____
_____

Entry: 17
Date: ___/___/___

> *If you want to conquer the anxiety of life, live in the moment, live in the breath.*
> **– Amit Ray**

What's happening in my life right now?
_____
_____

What's my dream goal?
_____
_____

What am I grateful for today?
_____
_____

What did I do today that I am proud of?
_____
_____

What is one thing I can learn or improve?
_____
_____

How did I L.E.A.D. today?
_____
_____

WIN: What's important now?
_____
_____

Entry: 18
Date: ___/___/___

> *Think about every good thing in your life right now. Free yourself of worrying. Let go of the anxiety, breathe. Stay positive, all is well.*
> **– Germany Kent**

What's happening in my life right now?
_____
_____

What's my dream goal?
_____
_____

What am I grateful for today?
_____
_____

What did I do today that I am proud of?
_____
_____

What is one thing I can learn or improve?
_____
_____

How did I L.E.A.D. today?
_____
_____

WIN: What's important now?
_____
_____

Daily Reflection

Entry: 19
Date: ___/___/___

Concentration is a fine antidote to anxiety.
– **Jack Nicklaus**

What's happening in my life right now?
_____
_____

What's my dream goal?
_____
_____

What am I grateful for today?
_____
_____

What did I do today that I am proud of?
_____
_____

What is one thing I can learn or improve?
_____
_____

How did I L.E.A.D. today?
_____
_____

WIN: What's important now?
_____
_____

Entry: 20

Date: ___/___/___

> *Breathing in, I calm body and mind. Breathing out, I smile. Dwelling in the present moment, I know this is a wonderful moment.*
> **- Thich Nhat Hanh**

What's happening in my life right now?

_____

_____

What's my dream goal?

_____

_____

What am I grateful for today?

_____

_____

What did I do today that I am proud of?

_____

_____

What is one thing I can learn or improve?

_____

_____

How did I L.E.A.D. today?

_____

_____

WIN: What's important now?

_____

_____

Daily Reflection

Entry: 21
Date: ___/___/___

When life is foggy, the path is unclear, and mind is dull, remember your breath. It has the power to give you peace.
– Amit Ray

What's happening in my life right now?
___
___

What's my dream goal?
___
___

What am I grateful for today?
___
___

What did I do today that I am proud of?
___
___

What is one thing I can learn or improve?
___
___

How did I L.E.A.D. today?
___
___

WIN: What's important now?
___
___

#TRAINTHEMENTALGAME

WEEKLY REFLECTION

Daily Reflection

> *Don't place your mistakes on your head. Their weight may crush you. Instead, place them under your feet and use them as a platform to view your horizons.*
> **– Unknown**

Challenge 3: Release a Poor Performance

This week's challenge is to let go of a poor performance or mistake. Too often, athletes hold onto a poor past performance. It's like a lousy highlight reel that keeps replaying itself over and over in your mind.

It's time to let it go. Use a separate piece of paper to complete this exercise.

- Set a timer for 5 minutes.
- Write about that poor performance or that event.
- Describe it.
- Why does it haunt you?
- Why is it so important?
- How does it make you feel?
- Don't think too hard. Just write.

When the timer goes off, look at the page. Then tear it into pieces and throw it away.

That performance or event is over. It is time to let it go. This journal is about the present moment.

It is about being your best self today.

What's one thing you will do differently this week?

Entry: 22
Date: ___/___/___

It's not whether you get knocked down, it's whether you get up.
— **Vince Lombardi**

What's happening in my life right now?
_____
_____

What's my dream goal?
_____
_____

What am I grateful for today?
_____
_____

What did I do today that I am proud of?
_____
_____

What is one thing I can learn or improve?
_____
_____

How did I L.E.A.D. today?
_____
_____

WIN: What's important now?
_____
_____

Daily Reflection

Entry: 23
Date: ___/___/___

> *I've failed over and over and over again in my life. And that is why I succeed.*
> **– Michael Jordan**

What's happening in my life right now?
_____
_____

What's my dream goal?
_____
_____

What am I grateful for today?
_____
_____

What did I do today that I am proud of?
_____
_____

What is one thing I can learn or improve?
_____
_____

How did I L.E.A.D. today?
_____
_____

WIN: What's important now?
_____
_____

Entry: 24
Date: ___/___/___

> *Doubt kills more dreams than failure ever will.*
> **– Suzy Kassem**

What's happening in my life right now?
_____
_____

What's my dream goal?
_____
_____

What am I grateful for today?
_____
_____

What did I do today that I am proud of?
_____
_____

What is one thing I can learn or improve?
_____
_____

How did I L.E.A.D. today?
_____
_____

WIN: What's important now?
_____
_____

Entry: 25
Date: ___/___/___

> *You will make mistakes. Learn from them.*
> — **David Beckham**

What's happening in my life right now?
_____
_____

What's my dream goal?
_____
_____

What am I grateful for today?
_____
_____

What did I do today that I am proud of?
_____
_____

What is one thing I can learn or improve?
_____
_____

How did I L.E.A.D. today?
_____
_____

WIN: What's important now?
_____
_____

Entry: 26
Date: ___/___/___

> *There is great power in letting go, and there is great freedom in moving on.*
> **– Unknown**

What's happening in my life right now?
_____
_____

What's my dream goal?
_____
_____

What am I grateful for today?
_____
_____

What did I do today that I am proud of?
_____
_____

What is one thing I can learn or improve?
_____
_____

How did I L.E.A.D. today?
_____
_____

WIN: What's important now?
_____
_____

Daily Reflection

Entry: 27
Date: ___/___/___

> *At times I think, "Why should I push myself?" But then I think, "How will I ever know how good I could have been?"*
> **– Michelle Kwan**

What's happening in my life right now?
_____
_____

What's my dream goal?
_____
_____

What am I grateful for today?
_____
_____

What did I do today that I am proud of?
_____
_____

What is one thing I can learn or improve?
_____
_____

How did I L.E.A.D. today?
_____
_____

WIN: What's important now?
_____
_____

Entry: 28
Date: ___/___/___

> *There's no substitute for hard work. If you work hard and prepare yourself, you might get beat, but you'll never lose.*
> **– Nancy Lieberman**

What's happening in my life right now?
_____
_____

What's my dream goal?
_____
_____

What am I grateful for today?
_____
_____

What did I do today that I am proud of?
_____
_____

What is one thing I can learn or improve?
_____
_____

How did I L.E.A.D. today?
_____
_____

WIN: What's important now?
_____
_____

WEEKLY REFLECTION

> *Your beliefs become your thoughts. Your thoughts become your words. Your words become your actions. Your actions become your habits. Your habits become your values. Your values become your destiny.*
> **– Unknown**

Challenge 4: Rewrite Limiting Beliefs

Limiting beliefs adversely impact our potential and performance. Limiting beliefs show up in our self-talk: "I am not good enough." "What if I fail?"

Write down three limiting beliefs you have (e.g., I'm not good enough):

1. _____
2. _____
3. _____

Now, rewrite them as affirmations or positive statements about who you are and who you are becoming (e.g., I train hard, I'm ready, I got this):

1. _____
2. _____
3. _____

If you are working towards a goal or a new skill, that means you are learning, and you just have not achieved it YET!

What's one thing you will do differently this week?

Entry: 29
Date: ___/___/___

> *All that we are is the result of what we have thought.*
> **– Buddha**

What's happening in my life right now?
_____
_____

What's my dream goal?
_____
_____

What am I grateful for today?
_____
_____

What did I do today that I am proud of?
_____
_____

What is one thing I can learn or improve?
_____
_____

How did I L.E.A.D. today?
_____
_____

WIN: What's important now?
_____
_____

Entry: 30
Date: ___/___/___

> *If you hear a voice within you say 'you cannot paint,' then by all means paint, and that voice will be silenced.*
> **– Vincent Van Gogh**

What's happening in my life right now?
_____
_____

What's my dream goal?
_____
_____

What am I grateful for today?
_____
_____

What did I do today that I am proud of?
_____
_____

What is one thing I can learn or improve?
_____
_____

How did I L.E.A.D. today?
_____
_____

WIN: What's important now?
_____
_____

Daily Reflection

Entry: 31
Date: ___/___/___

> *Believe you can, and you're halfway there.*
> **– Theodore Roosevelt**

What's happening in my life right now?
_____
_____

What's my dream goal?
_____
_____

What am I grateful for today?
_____
_____

What did I do today that I am proud of?
_____
_____

What is one thing I can learn or improve?
_____
_____

How did I L.E.A.D. today?
_____
_____

WIN: What's important now?
_____
_____

#TRAINTHEMENTALGAME

Entry: 32
Date: ___/___/___

> *The mind is the limit. As long as the mind can envision the fact that you can do something, you can do it, as long as you really believe 100 percent.*
> **– Arnold Schwarzenegger**

What's happening in my life right now?
_____
_____

What's my dream goal?
_____
_____

What am I grateful for today?
_____
_____

What did I do today that I am proud of?
_____
_____

What is one thing I can learn or improve?
_____
_____

How did I L.E.A.D. today?
_____
_____

WIN: What's important now?
_____
_____

Daily Reflection

Entry: 33
Date: ___/___/___

If you can believe it, the mind can achieve it.
— **Ronnie Lott**

What's happening in my life right now?
_____
_____

What's my dream goal?
_____
_____

What am I grateful for today?
_____
_____

What did I do today that I am proud of?
_____
_____

What is one thing I can learn or improve?
_____
_____

How did I L.E.A.D. today?
_____
_____

WIN: What's important now?
_____
_____

Entry: 34
Date: ___/___/___

You just can't beat the person who never gives up.
— **Babe Ruth**

What's happening in my life right now?
_____
_____

What's my dream goal?
_____
_____

What am I grateful for today?
_____
_____

What did I do today that I am proud of?
_____
_____

What is one thing I can learn or improve?
_____
_____

How did I L.E.A.D. today?
_____
_____

WIN: What's important now?
_____
_____

Daily Reflection

Entry: 35
Date: ___/___/___

> *Feed your faith, and your fear will starve to death.*
> — **Unknown**

What's happening in my life right now?
_____
_____

What's my dream goal?
_____
_____

What am I grateful for today?
_____
_____

What did I do today that I am proud of?
_____
_____

What is one thing I can learn or improve?
_____
_____

How did I L.E.A.D. today?
_____
_____

WIN: What's important now?
_____
_____

WEEKLY REFLECTION

> *The ability to conquer oneself is no doubt the most precious of all things sports bestows.*
> — **Olga Korbut**

Challenge 5: Let Go of Unrealistic Expectations

Five weeks — you're making great progress. Congratulations! Keep it up.

Personal expectations in sports are different from goals. According to the Merriam-Webster dictionary, a goal is the end toward which effort is directed.

In contrast, personal expectations are standards of performance that we hold ourselves to. These may or may not be realistic. If we don't achieve them, they can erode our confidence and performance.

What expectations do you have for your performance (e.g., scores, times, results, etc.)? List 3-5. (I have to get a personal record, I have to win my race, I have to score 15 points, etc.)

1. _____
2. _____
3. _____
4. _____
5. _____

What happens when you don't achieve your expectations?

_____

_____

_____

_____

_____

This week, shift your focus from the outcome to the process of competing well. For example, in basketball, the process could be focused on being aggressive, boxing out, denying passes, and hustling after every loose ball. For the expectations you listed earlier, how can you shift your focus to the process?

_____

_____

_____

_____

_____

Entry: 36

Date: ___/___/___

> *I'm not in this world to live up to your expectations and you're not in this world to live up to mine.*
> — **Bruce Lee**

What's happening in my life right now?
___
___

What's my dream goal?
___
___

What am I grateful for today?
___
___

What did I do today that I am proud of?
___
___

What is one thing I can learn or improve?
___
___

How did I L.E.A.D. today?
___
___

WIN: What's important now?
___
___

Entry: 37

Date: ___/___/___

Hard work beats talent when talent fails to work hard.
— **Tim Notke**

What's happening in my life right now?
_____
_____

What's my dream goal?
_____
_____

What am I grateful for today?
_____
_____

What did I do today that I am proud of?
_____
_____

What is one thing I can learn or improve?
_____
_____

How did I L.E.A.D. today?
_____
_____

WIN: What's important now?
_____
_____

Daily Reflection

Entry: 38
Date: ___/___/___

Be patient and trust the process.
— Unknown

What's happening in my life right now?
_____
_____

What's my dream goal?
_____
_____

What am I grateful for today?
_____
_____

What did I do today that I am proud of?
_____
_____

What is one thing I can learn or improve?
_____
_____

How did I L.E.A.D. today?
_____
_____

WIN: What's important now?
_____
_____

Entry: 39
Date: ___/___/___

> *I have failed many times, but I have never gone into a game expecting myself to fail.*
> **– Michael Jordan**

What's happening in my life right now?
_____
_____

What's my dream goal?
_____
_____

What am I grateful for today?
_____
_____

What did I do today that I am proud of?
_____
_____

What is one thing I can learn or improve?
_____
_____

How did I L.E.A.D. today?
_____
_____

WIN: What's important now?
_____
_____

Daily Reflection

Entry: 40
Date: ___/___/___

Always make a total effort, even when the odds are against you.
— **Arnold Palmer**

What's happening in my life right now?
_____
_____

What's my dream goal?
_____
_____

What am I grateful for today?
_____
_____

What did I do today that I am proud of?
_____
_____

What is one thing I can learn or improve?
_____
_____

How did I L.E.A.D. today?
_____
_____

WIN: What's important now?
_____
_____

Entry: 41
Date: ___/___/___

> *Don't worry about failures, worry about the chances you miss when you don't even try.*
> **– Jack Canfield**

What's happening in my life right now?
_____
_____

What's my dream goal?
_____
_____

What am I grateful for today?
_____
_____

What did I do today that I am proud of?
_____
_____

What is one thing I can learn or improve?
_____
_____

How did I L.E.A.D. today?
_____
_____

WIN: What's important now?
_____
_____

Daily Reflection

Entry: 42
Date: ___/___/___

> *If you don't love what you do, you won't do it with much conviction or passion.*
> **– Mia Hamm**

What's happening in my life right now?
_____
_____

What's my dream goal?
_____
_____

What am I grateful for today?
_____
_____

What did I do today that I am proud of?
_____
_____

What is one thing I can learn or improve?
_____
_____

How did I L.E.A.D. today?
_____
_____

WIN: What's important now?
_____
_____

WEEKLY REFLECTION

Champions keep playing until they get it right.
— **Billie Jean King**

Challenge 6: Commit to Improvement

You've made it to week six! Nice job! Keep it up.

The challenge this week is to focus on the process of improvement. Continue to shift your focus from the outcome (e.g., I have to win, I have to score, I have to beat my record, etc.) to the process of improvement. It can be challenging to retrain your mind — you may have spent years focusing on the outcome. The key, however, is to focus on improving. What is one area of improvement that you can focus on this week?

_____

_____

Why did you choose this area?

_____

_____

What happens to your stress when you focus on improvement versus an outcome?

_____

_____

_____

A series of small improvements can lead to significant gains.

Entry: 43
Date: ___/___/___

> *The difference between a winner and a loser is, many times, a matter of inches. If you think you can do it, most of the time you'll do it.*
> **– Nancy Lieberman**

What's happening in my life right now?
_____
_____

What's my dream goal?
_____
_____

What am I grateful for today?
_____
_____

What did I do today that I am proud of?
_____
_____

What is one thing I can learn or improve?
_____
_____

How did I L.E.A.D. today?
_____
_____

WIN: What's important now?
_____
_____

Daily Reflection

Entry: 44
Date: ___/___/___

Don't complain. Just work harder.
— Jacki Robinson

What's happening in my life right now?
_____
_____

What's my dream goal?
_____
_____

What am I grateful for today?
_____
_____

What did I do today that I am proud of?
_____
_____

What is one thing I can learn or improve?
_____
_____

How did I L.E.A.D. today?
_____
_____

WIN: What's important now?
_____
_____

Entry: 45
Date: ___/___/___

> *If you persevere long enough, if you do the right things long enough, the right things will happen.*
> **– Manon Rheaume**

What's happening in my life right now?
_____
_____

What's my dream goal?
_____
_____

What am I grateful for today?
_____
_____

What did I do today that I am proud of?
_____
_____

What is one thing I can learn or improve?
_____
_____

How did I L.E.A.D. today?
_____
_____

WIN: What's important now?
_____
_____

Daily Reflection

Entry: 46
Date: ___/___/___

Push harder than yesterday if you want a different tomorrow.
— **Unknown**

What's happening in my life right now?
_____
_____

What's my dream goal?
_____
_____

What am I grateful for today?
_____
_____

What did I do today that I am proud of?
_____
_____

What is one thing I can learn or improve?
_____
_____

How did I L.E.A.D. today?
_____
_____

WIN: What's important now?
_____
_____

Entry: 47

Date: ___/___/___

> *The more you focus on the results, the slower the process. The more you focus on the process, the faster the results.*
> **— Unknown**

What's happening in my life right now?

_____

_____

What's my dream goal?

_____

_____

What am I grateful for today?

_____

_____

What did I do today that I am proud of?

_____

_____

What is one thing I can learn or improve?

_____

_____

How did I L.E.A.D. today?

_____

_____

WIN: What's important now?

_____

_____

Daily Reflection

Entry: 48
Date: ___/___/___

> *Fall in love with the process and the results will come.*
> — **Eric Thomas**

What's happening in my life right now?
_____
_____

What's my dream goal?
_____
_____

What am I grateful for today?
_____
_____

What did I do today that I am proud of?
_____
_____

What is one thing I can learn or improve?
_____
_____

How did I L.E.A.D. today?
_____
_____

WIN: What's important now?
_____
_____

Entry: 49
Date: ___/___/___

> *Success is a journey, not a destination. Focus on the process.*
> **– Unknown**

What's happening in my life right now?
_____
_____

What's my dream goal?
_____
_____

What am I grateful for today?
_____
_____

What did I do today that I am proud of?
_____
_____

What is one thing I can learn or improve?
_____
_____

How did I L.E.A.D. today?
_____
_____

WIN: What's important now?
_____
_____

WEEKLY REFLECTION

> *A mistake should be your teacher, not your attacker. A mistake is a lesson, not a loss. It is a temporary necessary detour, not a dead end.*
>
> **– Unknown**

Challenge 7: Moving through Mistakes

Super effort! You are already in week seven and that shows a commitment to excellence.

This week your challenge is to focus on learning from mistakes and moving through errors. No one in sports at any level is perfect.

So many athletes fear failure. We can learn the most from our disappointments and our failures if we are open to learning. What can you learn from every win and defeat?

We can anticipate mistakes that will happen in every competition, at every level. For example, in basketball, we can predict that there will be:

- Missed shots
- Missed defensive assignments
- Bad passes
- Steals
- Bad shots
- Fouls
- Poor calls

Daily Reflection

List some mistakes that commonly happen in your sport. Then list how you react to those mistakes.

_____

_____

_____

How does your reaction impact your performance? Choose one:

- ☐ Helps my performance
- ☐ Hurts my performance
- ☐ Depends

If you were wearing the coach's hat, how would you coach your mistake?

_____

_____

_____

The goal with any mistake during competition is to let it go and to stay in the moment. After the competition, learn and continue to improve.

What will you focus on this week?

_____

_____

_____

Entry: 50

Date: ___/___/___

> *You can't always be the best. You have to remember that everyone makes mistakes sometimes.*
> **– Aly Raisman**

What's happening in my life right now?
_____
_____

What's my dream goal?
_____
_____

What am I grateful for today?
_____
_____

What did I do today that I am proud of?
_____
_____

What is one thing I can learn or improve?
_____
_____

How did I L.E.A.D. today?
_____
_____

WIN: What's important now?
_____
_____

Daily Reflection

Entry: 51
Date: ___/___/___

> *It's what you do with the rough patches that will define the athlete that you'll become.*
> **– Dana Vollmer**

What's happening in my life right now?
_____
_____

What's my dream goal?
_____
_____

What am I grateful for today?
_____
_____

What did I do today that I am proud of?
_____
_____

What is one thing I can learn or improve?
_____
_____

How did I L.E.A.D. today?
_____
_____

WIN: What's important now?
_____
_____

Entry: 52
Date: ___/___/___

> *What do you do with a mistake: recognize it, admit it, learn from it, forget it.*
> **– Dean Smith**

What's happening in my life right now?
_____
_____

What's my dream goal?
_____
_____

What am I grateful for today?
_____
_____

What did I do today that I am proud of?
_____
_____

What is one thing I can learn or improve?
_____
_____

How did I L.E.A.D. today?
_____
_____

WIN: What's important now?
_____
_____

Daily Reflection

Entry: 53
Date: ___/___/___

> *It's not how far you fall, but how high you bounce that counts.*
> **— Zig Ziglar**

What's happening in my life right now?
_____
_____

What's my dream goal?
_____
_____

What am I grateful for today?
_____
_____

What did I do today that I am proud of?
_____
_____

What is one thing I can learn or improve?
_____
_____

How did I L.E.A.D. today?
_____
_____

WIN: What's important now?
_____
_____

Entry: 54

Date: ___/___/___

> *Courage is being afraid but going on anyhow.*
> — Dan Rather

What's happening in my life right now?
_____
_____

What's my dream goal?
_____
_____

What am I grateful for today?
_____
_____

What did I do today that I am proud of?
_____
_____

What is one thing I can learn or improve?
_____
_____

How did I L.E.A.D. today?
_____
_____

WIN: What's important now?
_____
_____

Daily Reflection

Entry: 55
Date: ___/___/___

> *Survival can be summed up in three words — never give up. That's the heart of it really. Just keep trying.*
> **– Bear Grylls**

What's happening in my life right now?
_____
_____

What's my dream goal?
_____
_____

What am I grateful for today?
_____
_____

What did I do today that I am proud of?
_____
_____

What is one thing I can learn or improve?
_____
_____

How did I L.E.A.D. today?
_____
_____

WIN: What's important now?
_____
_____

#TRAINTHEMENTALGAME

Entry: 56
Date: ___/___/___

> *You have to remember that the hard days are what make you stronger. If you never had any bad days, you would never have that sense of accomplishment!*
> **– Aly Raisman**

What's happening in my life right now?
_____
_____

What's my dream goal?
_____
_____

What am I grateful for today?
_____
_____

What did I do today that I am proud of?
_____
_____

What is one thing I can learn or improve?
_____
_____

How did I L.E.A.D. today?
_____
_____

WIN: What's important now?
_____
_____

WEEKLY REFLECTION

> *Confidence is contagious. So is lack of confidence.*
> **– Vince Lombardi**

Challenge 8: Strategies to Strengthen Confidence

Week eight. You are doing great! This week's challenge is on confidence and the battle with self-doubt.

Almost everyone struggles with self-doubt at times. When you are in that spot, remember to play the part. Pull your shoulders back, and stand confident.

Confidence comes from within. What routine do you do that helps you be confident (e.g., making an effort when training, practicing self-care, etc.)? List at least three examples:

1. _____
2. _____
3. _____

Confidence also comes from others. What have coaches, opponents and teammates, said to you that fuels your confidence?

1. _____
2. _____
3. _____

Create a confidence resume. List all the reasons that you should feel confident (e.g., training, conditioning, awards, recognition).

1. _____

2. _____

3. _____

4. _____

5. _____

6. _____

7. _____

8. _____

9. _____

10. _____

What else can I use to help fuel my confidence? A meaningful video? A powerful quote? A screen saver of an inspiring photo?

Entry: 57

Date: ___/___/___

> *Optimism is the faith that leads to achievement. Nothing can be done without hope and confidence.*
> **– Helen Keller**

What's happening in my life right now?

_____

_____

What's my dream goal?

_____

_____

What am I grateful for today?

_____

_____

What did I do today that I am proud of?

_____

_____

What is one thing I can learn or improve?

_____

_____

How did I L.E.A.D. today?

_____

_____

WIN: What's important now?

_____

_____

Daily Reflection

Entry: 58

Date: ___/___/___

> *Change your thoughts, and you change your world.*
> **– Norman Vincent Peale**

What's happening in my life right now?
_____
_____

What's my dream goal?
_____
_____

What am I grateful for today?
_____
_____

What did I do today that I am proud of?
_____
_____

What is one thing I can learn or improve?
_____
_____

How did I L.E.A.D. today?
_____
_____

WIN: What's important now?
_____
_____

Entry: 59
Date: ___/___/___

> *The secrets of making dreams come true can be summarized in four Cs: curiosity, confidence, courage, and constancy.*
> **– Walt Disney**

What's happening in my life right now?
_____
_____

What's my dream goal?
_____
_____

What am I grateful for today?
_____
_____

What did I do today that I am proud of?
_____
_____

What is one thing I can learn or improve?
_____
_____

How did I L.E.A.D. today?
_____
_____

WIN: What's important now?
_____
_____

Entry: 60
Date: ___/___/___

> *With realization of one's own potential and self-confidence in one's ability, one can build a better world.*
> **– Dalai Lama**

What's happening in my life right now?
_____
_____

What's my dream goal?
_____
_____

What am I grateful for today?
_____
_____

What did I do today that I am proud of?
_____
_____

What is one thing I can learn or improve?
_____
_____

How did I L.E.A.D. today?
_____
_____

WIN: What's important now?
_____
_____

Entry: 61
Date: ___/___/___

> *I don't run away from a challenge because I am afraid. Instead, I run toward it because the only way to escape fear is to trample it beneath your feet.*
>
> **– Nadia Comăneci**

What's happening in my life right now?
_____
_____

What's my dream goal?
_____
_____

What am I grateful for today?
_____
_____

What did I do today that I am proud of?
_____
_____

What is one thing I can learn or improve?
_____
_____

How did I L.E.A.D. today?
_____
_____

WIN: What's important now?
_____
_____

Daily Reflection

Entry: 62
Date: ___/___/___

> *The vision of a champion is someone who is bent over, drenched in sweat, at the point of exhaustion, when nobody else is watching.*
> **– Anson Dorrance**

What's happening in my life right now?
_____
_____

What's my dream goal?
_____
_____

What am I grateful for today?
_____
_____

What did I do today that I am proud of?
_____
_____

What is one thing I can learn or improve?
_____
_____

How did I L.E.A.D. today?
_____
_____

WIN: What's important now?
_____
_____

Entry: 63

Date: ___/___/___

> *Always remember you are braver than you believe, stronger than you seem, and smarter than you think.*
> — **A. A. Milne**

What's happening in my life right now?
_____
_____

What's my dream goal?
_____
_____

What am I grateful for today?
_____
_____

What did I do today that I am proud of?
_____
_____

What is one thing I can learn or improve?
_____
_____

How did I L.E.A.D. today?
_____
_____

WIN: What's important now?
_____
_____

WEEKLY REFLECTION

> *Visualize. Picture yourself slaying it and becoming exactly what you want to be. If your mind can conceive it, you can be it. Hold a dress rehearsal for success in your mind.*
> **– Unknown**

Challenge 9: Visualize Your Success

Too often, our thoughts can become stuck on a mistake or a bad performance. It's time to retrain your brain and recreate a joyous moment in your sport — or envision one in the future.

Use the next page to write about and detail a triumphant past moment in your sport. Write about a successful moment from the past where everything aligned. You were happy with your performance and your confidence was strong.

Think about your uniform colors, the sounds of the crowd, details about the venue, the emotions you felt, and how your coaches and teammates reacted to your performance. After you write about it, close your eyes, take a few deep breaths, and mentally replay that moment in time.

Many athletes supplement their visualization efforts by watching highlight video from strong performances.

A college golfer I worked with mentally played a round of golf on his college course every day during his summer break. He envisioned himself birdieing every hole. When he returned to campus, he shot six strokes under par, his personal best round. Visualization can be a potent tool.

Another way to visualize is to see yourself competing well and with confidence in the future.

Daily Reflection

Describe your performance

_____
_____
_____
_____
_____
_____
_____
_____
_____
_____
_____
_____
_____
_____
_____

Take a few moments to visualize your success this week. Practice this skill before each training, practice, or competition.

Entry: 64
Date: ___/___/___

> *You are more productive by doing fifteen minutes of visualization than from sixteen hours of hard labor.*
> **— Abraham Hicks**

What's happening in my life right now?
_____
_____

What's my dream goal?
_____
_____

What am I grateful for today?
_____
_____

What did I do today that I am proud of?
_____
_____

What is one thing I can learn or improve?
_____
_____

How did I L.E.A.D. today?
_____
_____

WIN: What's important now?
_____
_____

Daily Reflection

Entry: 65

Date: ___/___/___

> *I would visualize things coming to me. It would just make me feel better. Visualization works if you work hard.*
> **– Jim Carrey**

What's happening in my life right now?
_____
_____

What's my dream goal?
_____
_____

What am I grateful for today?
_____
_____

What did I do today that I am proud of?
_____
_____

What is one thing I can learn or improve?
_____
_____

How did I L.E.A.D. today?
_____
_____

WIN: What's important now?
_____
_____

Entry: 66

Date: ___/___/___

> *If we all did the things we are capable of doing, we would literally astound ourselves.*
> **– Thomas Edison**

What's happening in my life right now?
_____
_____

What's my dream goal?
_____
_____

What am I grateful for today?
_____
_____

What did I do today that I am proud of?
_____
_____

What is one thing I can learn or improve?
_____
_____

How did I L.E.A.D. today?
_____
_____

WIN: What's important now?
_____
_____

Daily Reflection

Entry: 67

Date: ___/___/___

> *You can't do anything that you can't picture yourself doing. Once you make the picturing process conscious and deliberate, you begin to create the self you want to be.*
> **– Unknown**

What's happening in my life right now?
_____
_____

What's my dream goal?
_____
_____

What am I grateful for today?
_____
_____

What did I do today that I am proud of?
_____
_____

What is one thing I can learn or improve?
_____
_____

How did I L.E.A.D. today?
_____
_____

WIN: What's important now?
_____
_____

Entry: 68
Date: ___/___/___

> *I believe that visualization is one of the most powerful means of achieving personal goals.*
> **— Harvey Mackay**

What's happening in my life right now?
_____
_____

What's my dream goal?
_____
_____

What am I grateful for today?
_____
_____

What did I do today that I am proud of?
_____
_____

What is one thing I can learn or improve?
_____
_____

How did I L.E.A.D. today?
_____
_____

WIN: What's important now?
_____
_____

Daily Reflection

Entry: 69
Date: ___/___/___

> *I go to bed every night thinking about all the possible ways I can succeed.*
> **— Ronda Rousey**

What's happening in my life right now?
_____
_____

What's my dream goal?
_____
_____

What am I grateful for today?
_____
_____

What did I do today that I am proud of?
_____
_____

What is one thing I can learn or improve?
_____
_____

How did I L.E.A.D. today?
_____
_____

WIN: What's important now?
_____
_____

Entry: 70
Date: ___/___/___

> *Even coal takes over a billion years to become a diamond. Don't be so hard on yourself.*
> **– Chris Butler**

What's happening in my life right now?
_____
_____

What's my dream goal?
_____
_____

What am I grateful for today?
_____
_____

What did I do today that I am proud of?
_____
_____

What is one thing I can learn or improve?
_____
_____

How did I L.E.A.D. today?
_____
_____

WIN: What's important now?
_____
_____

WEEKLY REFLECTION

> *Learn to control your emotions, or they will control you.*
> – Edgar Martínez

Challenge 10: Emotional Control in Sports

At the US Open, Novak Djokovic was disqualified when a ball he hit in frustration struck a line judge. The U.S. Open top-seeded player lost control, and it cost him.

Emotional control in sports matters. Earlier, you did an exercise to identify what mistakes or events are most likely to happen in your sport and how you react to each of them. During competition, the best response is no response. The goal is to stay in the moment. How do we learn to do that?

1. Have a mistake ritual. After you make a mistake, brush it off or flush it, then reset by moving on to the next play or event. Access the YouTube videos by the Positive Coaching Alliance for examples of mistake rituals.
2. Count backward — 5, 4, 3, 2, 1 — and blast the mistake out of your mind. Then tell yourself to focus on the next play, next moment, next ball — whatever is appropriate to your sport.
3. Use R3, an approach I learned from Dr. Patrick Cohn. Recognize your response: Regroup; Refocus.
4. Acknowledge that no one in any sport is perfect. Your mistake is the same mistake that college, professional, and Olympic athletes make. Permit yourself to be human.

Daily Reflection

Entry: 71
Date: ___/___/___

> *Things turn out best for the people who make the best of the way things turn out.*
> **– John Wooden**

What's happening in my life right now?
_____
_____

What's my dream goal?
_____
_____

What am I grateful for today?
_____
_____

What did I do today that I am proud of?
_____
_____

What is one thing I can learn or improve?
_____
_____

How did I L.E.A.D. today?
_____
_____

WIN: What's important now?
_____
_____

Entry: 72
Date: ___/___/___

> *Failure happens all the time. It happens every day in practice. What makes you better is how you react to it.*
> **– Mia Hamm**

What's happening in my life right now?
_____
_____

What's my dream goal?
_____
_____

What am I grateful for today?
_____
_____

What did I do today that I am proud of?
_____
_____

What is one thing I can learn or improve?
_____
_____

How did I L.E.A.D. today?
_____
_____

WIN: What's important now?
_____
_____

Daily Reflection

Entry: 73
Date: ___/___/___

> *A lot of people think I am cold and have no feelings. But I do. I just try very hard to focus and not let my emotions take over on the golf course.*
> **–Annika Sörenstam**

What's happening in my life right now?
_____
_____

What's my dream goal?
_____
_____

What am I grateful for today?
_____
_____

What did I do today that I am proud of?
_____
_____

What is one thing I can learn or improve?
_____
_____

How did I L.E.A.D. today?
_____
_____

WIN: What's important now?
_____
_____

Entry: 74
Date: ___/___/___

> *A ballplayer who loses his head, who can't keep his cool, is worse than no ballplayer at all.*
> **– Lou Gehrig**

What's happening in my life right now?
_____
_____

What's my dream goal?
_____
_____

What am I grateful for today?
_____
_____

What did I do today that I am proud of?
_____
_____

What is one thing I can learn or improve?
_____
_____

How did I L.E.A.D. today?
_____
_____

WIN: What's important now?
_____
_____

Entry: 75
Date: ___/___/___

> *Don't practice until you get it right.*
> *Practice until you can't get it wrong.*
> — **Unknown**

What's happening in my life right now?
_____
_____

What's my dream goal?
_____
_____

What am I grateful for today?
_____
_____

What did I do today that I am proud of?
_____
_____

What is one thing I can learn or improve?
_____
_____

How did I L.E.A.D. today?
_____
_____

WIN: What's important now?
_____
_____

Entry: 76
Date: ___/___/___

> *As you walk down the fairway of life you must smell the roses, for you only get to play one round.*
> **– Ben Hogan**

What's happening in my life right now?
_____
_____

What's my dream goal?
_____
_____

What am I grateful for today?
_____
_____

What did I do today that I am proud of?
_____
_____

What is one thing I can learn or improve?
_____
_____

How did I L.E.A.D. today?
_____
_____

WIN: What's important now?
_____
_____

Daily Reflection

Entry: 77
Date: ___/___/___

> *When you react, you let others control you. When you respond, you are in control.*
> **– Bohdi Sanders**

What's happening in my life right now?
_____
_____

What's my dream goal?
_____
_____

What am I grateful for today?
_____
_____

What did I do today that I am proud of?
_____
_____

What is one thing I can learn or improve?
_____
_____

How did I L.E.A.D. today?
_____
_____

WIN: What's important now?
_____
_____

WEEKLY REFLECTION

Daily Reflection

> *One important key to success is self-confidence. An important key to self-confidence is preparation.*
> — **Arthur Ashe**

Challenge 11: 7 Steps to Mentally Prepare

Congratulations on putting in the work thus far. You're building skills and habits that will pay dividends — personally, professionally, and athletically.

This week's challenge is to level up your mental preparation for practice and competition. How you prepare matters.

According to NFL safety Bo Eason, all-time great NFL receiver Jerry Rice had an incredible work ethic. In every drill at football practice, Jerry Rice ALWAYS went full speed and ran the ball into the end zone on every routine. Why? He believed every time his hands caught the football, his feet were going into the end zone. His practice mindset fueled his success.

This week, implement the seven steps to mentally prepare for sports, adapted from Dr. Patrick Cohn's Athlete's Mental Edge Workbook "Mental Game Strategies for Pregame Preparation."

1. Enter the role of a competitive athlete. Be where your feet are. Park any distractions until after your practice or competition.
2. Let go of unrealistic expectations. No one is perfect.
3. Be proactive with your confidence. Have a mantra: I've got this. I have trained for this. I am ready. I'm prepared. I am capable.

4. Focus on the process of competing well. L.E.A.D. Identify keywords for your sport and associate them with your performance. Examples:
   - **Basketball**: be aggressive, box out, drive to the basket.
   - **Baseball**: good swing, good contact, stay low.
   - **Soccer**: be aggressive, follow the ball, stay in the play.
   - **Swimming**: Strong start, strong stroke, strong kick, strong turn.
5. Mentally rehearse your performance. See and feel yourself competing well and with confidence.
6. Trust your training. You are prepared for today. Don't judge your warm-up. Your warm-up is to ready your body physically for competition. It does not set the stage for success or failure.
7. Embrace your nerves. They are a sign that you are ready to compete. Channel your extra energy into a strong start to your competition.

And have fun!

This week, be intentional about how you prepare mentally for sport.

Reorder your journal now.

Daily Reflection

Entry: 78
Date: ___/___/___

> *It's not the will to win that matters — everyone has that. It's the will to prepare to win that matters.*
> **– Paul "Bear" Bryant**

What's happening in my life right now?
_____
_____

What's my dream goal?
_____
_____

What am I grateful for today?
_____
_____

What did I do today that I am proud of?
_____
_____

What is one thing I can learn or improve?
_____
_____

How did I L.E.A.D. today?
_____
_____

WIN: What's important now?
_____
_____

Entry: 79
Date: ___/___/___

> *Your body can do it. It's time to convince your mind.*
> **– Unknown**

What's happening in my life right now?
_____
_____

What's my dream goal?
_____
_____

What am I grateful for today?
_____
_____

What did I do today that I am proud of?
_____
_____

What is one thing I can learn or improve?
_____
_____

How did I L.E.A.D. today?
_____
_____

WIN: What's important now?
_____
_____

Daily Reflection

Entry: 80
Date: ___/___/___

If you fail to prepare, you're prepared to fail.
— **Mark Spitz**

What's happening in my life right now?
_____
_____

What's my dream goal?
_____
_____

What am I grateful for today?
_____
_____

What did I do today that I am proud of?
_____
_____

What is one thing I can learn or improve?
_____
_____

How did I L.E.A.D. today?
_____
_____

WIN: What's important now?
_____
_____

#TRAINTHEMENTALGAME

Entry: 81
Date: ___/___/___

> *Success is where preparation and opportunity meet.*
> **– Bobby Unser**

What's happening in my life right now?
_____
_____

What's my dream goal?
_____
_____

What am I grateful for today?
_____
_____

What did I do today that I am proud of?
_____
_____

What is one thing I can learn or improve?
_____
_____

How did I L.E.A.D. today?
_____
_____

WIN: What's important now?
_____
_____

Daily Reflection

Entry: 82
Date: ___/___/___

> *Until you are mentally ready, you will never be physically prepared.*
> **– Unknown**

What's happening in my life right now?
_____
_____

What's my dream goal?
_____
_____

What am I grateful for today?
_____
_____

What did I do today that I am proud of?
_____
_____

What is one thing I can learn or improve?
_____
_____

How did I L.E.A.D. today?
_____
_____

WIN: What's important now?
_____
_____

Entry: 83

Date: ___/___/___

> *Mentally prepare and then physically dominate.*
> **- Unknown**

What's happening in my life right now?
___
___

What's my dream goal?
___
___

What am I grateful for today?
___
___

What did I do today that I am proud of?
___
___

What is one thing I can learn or improve?
___
___

How did I L.E.A.D. today?
___
___

WIN: What's important now?
___
___

Daily Reflection

Entry: 84
Date: ___/___/___

> *My thoughts before a big race are usually pretty simple. I tell myself: Get out of the blocks, run your race, stay relaxed.*
> **– Carl Lewis**

What's happening in my life right now?
_____
_____

What's my dream goal?
_____
_____

What am I grateful for today?
_____
_____

What did I do today that I am proud of?
_____
_____

What is one thing I can learn or improve?
_____
_____

How did I L.E.A.D. today?
_____
_____

WIN: What's important now?
_____
_____

Weekly Reflection

> *Success comes from knowing that you did your best to become the best that you are capable of becoming.*
> **– John Wooden**

Challenge 12: Your Sport and Your Identity

Sports are what you do, not who you are. Though your sport might be a big part of your life, it's important to realize that there are other components to your identity.

Athletes can feel the pressure of potentially disappointing others — teammates, coaches, parents, fans. Those closest to you know how hard you work and what your goals are. If you fall short of your dreams, others will be disappointed FOR you, not IN you.

Think about all the pieces of your life. Are you a brother/sister/daughter/son? Do you like music or play an instrument? Are you good at math, science, art? Do you attend church or other group events? What are your interests and talents?

Your identity comprises all the components of your life, in addition to sports.

On the next page, fill in the circle with the different parts of your life, being sure to reflect both who you are and what you do. Your picture is unique to you.

Example:

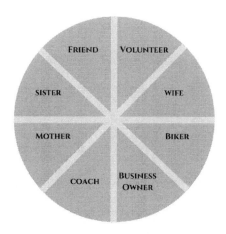

My Identity:

Know that you are loved. Your are "enough" regardless of how you perform in your sport. Remind yourself of this daily.

Daily Reflection

Entry: 85
Date: ___/___/___

> *Remembering who you are is how you take your power back.*
> **— Lalah Delia**

What's happening in my life right now?
_____
_____

What's my dream goal?
_____
_____

What am I grateful for today?
_____
_____

What did I do today that I am proud of?
_____
_____

What is one thing I can learn or improve?
_____
_____

How did I L.E.A.D. today?
_____
_____

WIN: What's important now?
_____
_____

Entry: 86
Date: ___/___/___

> *Success is not so much what we have as it is what we are.*
> — **Jim Rohn**

What's happening in my life right now?
_____
_____

What's my dream goal?
_____
_____

What am I grateful for today?
_____
_____

What did I do today that I am proud of?
_____
_____

What is one thing I can learn or improve?
_____
_____

How did I L.E.A.D. today?
_____
_____

WIN: What's important now?
_____
_____

Daily Reflection

Entry: 87
Date: ___/___/___

> *True champions aren't always the ones who win, but those with the most guts.*
> **– Mia Hamm**

What's happening in my life right now?
_____
_____

What's my dream goal?
_____
_____

What am I grateful for today?
_____
_____

What did I do today that I am proud of?
_____
_____

What is one thing I can learn or improve?
_____
_____

How did I L.E.A.D. today?
_____
_____

WIN: What's important now?
_____
_____

Entry: 88
Date: ___/___/___

> *Don't let a win get to your head or a loss to your heart.*
> **- Unknown**

What's happening in my life right now?
_____
_____

What's my dream goal?
_____
_____

What am I grateful for today?
_____
_____

What did I do today that I am proud of?
_____
_____

What is one thing I can learn or improve?
_____
_____

How did I L.E.A.D. today?
_____
_____

WIN: What's important now?
_____
_____

Daily Reflection

Entry: 89
Date: ___/___/___

> *What you get by achieving your goals is not as important as what you become by achieving your goals.*
> **– Zig Ziglar**

What's happening in my life right now?
_____
_____

What's my dream goal?
_____
_____

What am I grateful for today?
_____
_____

What did I do today that I am proud of?
_____
_____

What is one thing I can learn or improve?
_____
_____

How did I L.E.A.D. today?
_____
_____

WIN: What's important now?
_____
_____

Entry: 90

Date: ___/___/___

> *You must be the change you wish to see in the world.*
> — **Mahatma Gandhi**

What's happening in my life right now?
_____
_____

What's my dream goal?
_____
_____

What am I grateful for today?
_____
_____

What did I do today that I am proud of?
_____
_____

What is one thing I can learn or improve?
_____
_____

How did I L.E.A.D. today?
_____
_____

WIN: What's important now?
_____
_____

Weekly Reflection

Congratulations!

You have completed your **Great Sports Minds Athlete Journal**. Journaling is a valuable tool that can provide clarity throughout many aspects of your life.

Hopefully, you found the daily journal exercises and weekly challenges valuable. Reflecting and being intentional about your day, your sport, and your life are essential skills.

To be an athlete, you have to physically train hard. By using the **Great Sports Minds Athlete Journal** you trained your mindset.

For 90 days, you:

- Wrote your dreams as if you achieved them.
- Expressed gratitude.
- Shared moments of pride.
- Worked to improve and learn.
- Increased your daily focus.
- Committed to L.E.A.D.
- Learned essential mental performance skills.

You should be proud of your efforts. When you train for 90 days, you build new habits and new skills. Be sure to continue to invest in your personal development.

Great Sports Minds are trained. If you are interested in taking your mental performance training further, visit www.greatsportsmindsllc.com to access additional resources.

Online Resources

- **Great Sports Minds to Go** is mental performance training for today's busy athletes. The program consists of 13 short 1- to 5-minute videos and exercises that are accessible from any device. The training teaches mental performance skills that are used by today's top athletes.

- **Athlete Meditations** consists of three guided meditations to help you overcome the unique challenges that athletes face.

SPECIAL BONUS: sample our online course and our popular meditation, Letting Go, by scanning this QR Code.

Team or Small Group Coaching

Join other like-minded individuals (choose from athlete and coach sessions)for group coaching as you work through **Great Sports Minds to Go** and the **Athlete Meditations** programs. Learn how others apply these techniques and benefit from tools to improve performance.

One-on-One Coaching

Work 1:1 with Ann Zaprazny, Certified Mental Game Coach, to grow your mental performance skills. Various options are available. Schedule a free 15-minute consultation via my website www.greatsportsmindsllc.com.

Speaking Engagements

Book Ann Zaprazny to speak at one of your events in person or virtually. Email Ann at AnnZ@athlete-mentaltraining.com.

Quote Acknowledgments

Special thanks to those who contributed their favorite sports quote for inclusion in the **Great Sports Minds Journal.**

Jason Ardnt

Beth Boland

Michell Willard Hoffer

Jill Miller McGrorty

Anne Marie Schupper

Maddie Serfass

Geralyn Umstead Singer

Victoria Tredinnick

Frank Velasquez Jr.

Dino Warble

Walt Woltman

Book Recommendations

There are many books on mental performance. Below are a few of my favorites:

The Mindful Athlete: Secrets to Pure Performance by George Mumford

Mind Gym: An Athlete's Guide to Inner Excellence by Gary Mack

Burn Your Goals: The Counter Cultural Approach to Achieving Your Greatest Potential by Joshua Medcalf and Jamie Gilbert

The Champion's Mind: How Great Athletes Think, Train, and Thrive by Jim Afremow and Jim Craig

Relentless: From Good to Great to Unstoppable by Tim S. Grover

Grit: The Power of Passion and Perseverance by Angela Duckworth

Mindset: The New Psychology of Success by Carol S. Dweck

High-Performance Habits: How Extraordinary People Become That Way by Brendon Burchard

There's No Plan B for Your A-Game: Be the Best in the World at What You Do by Bo Eason

References

"CDC — How Much Sleep Do I Need? — Sleep and Sleep Disorders." Centers for Disease Control and Prevention, 2 Mar. 2017, www.cdc.gov/sleep/about_sleep/how_much_sleep.html.

Cohn, Patrick. "Athlete's Mental Edge Workbook: Mental Game Strategies for Coping with Mistakes." Peak Performance Sports, LLC, 2018.

Cohn, Patrick. "Athlete's Mental Edge Workbook: Mental Game Strategies for Overcoming High Expectations." Peak Performance Sports, LLC, 2018.

Cohn, Patrick. "Athlete's Mental Edge Workbook: Mental Game Strategies for Superior Confidence." Peak Performance Sports, LLC, 2018.

Cohn, Patrick. "Athlete's Mental Edge Workbook: Pregame Warmup." Peak Performance Sports, LLC. 2018.

Jacobo, Julia. "Teens Spend More than 7 Hours on Screens for Entertainment a Day: Report." ABC News, ABC News Network, 29 Oct. 2019, 2:06 pm, abcnews.go.com/US/teens-spend-hours-screens-entertainment-day-report/story?id=66607555.

Miller, Kori D. "14 Health Benefits of Practicing Gratitude According to Science." PositivePsychology.com, 1 Sept. 2020, positivepsychology.com/benefits-of-gratitude/.

Robbins, Mel. "Mel Robbins: 5 Second Rule." www.youtube.com/watch?v=nI2VQ-ZsNr0&t=237s, 7 Aug. 2014, www.youtube.com/watch?v=nI2VQ-ZsNr0&t=237s.

About the Author

Connect with Ann on any platform, email, or call her. She loves helping others succeed.

Visit www.greatsportsmindsllc.com for additional resources.

- Champion Mindset Questionnaire
- Online Training Programs:
  - **Great Sports Minds to Go** – Mental performance training program
  - **Athlete Meditations** – Custom athlete meditations
- Small Group Coaching
- Team Workshops
- Mastery 1:1 Coaching
- Speaking Engagements

Let's stay connected.

Ann Zaprazny

717-419-5789

AnnZ@Athletementaltraining.com

Twitter@AZaprazny

LinkedIn Ann Zaprazny

Instagram @GreatSportsMinds

Facebook@GreatSportsMinds

YouTube Ann Zaprazny

Made in the USA
Middletown, DE
13 March 2025